Five Life Poisons

Five Life Poisons

Managing the Obstacles and Negativities of Your Life

Deborah Peteler

FOREWORD BY
LATRI NYIMA DAKPA RINPOCHE

Dream Abbey
4 Covewood Court
Arden, NC 28704 USA
dreamabbey.com

© 2025 Deborah Peteler. All rights reserved.

Five Life Poisons is a registered trademark of Deborah Peteler in the United States.

No part of this book may be reproduced or translated in any form or by any means, electronic or mechanical, including photography, recording, or by any information storage and retrieval system or technologies now known or later developed, without permission in writing from the publisher.

Library of Congress Control Number: 2025936399

ISBN 978-1-951105-12-9 (paperback)
ISBN 978-1-951105-13-6 (ebook)

Contents

Foreword vii

Acknowledgement xi

Introduction 1

Anger 15

Attachment 25

Ignorance 37

Ego 47

Jealousy 57

Acknowledging the Five Life Poisons 67

Applying Wisdom as the Antidote 73

About Deborah Peteler 85

Notes 87

Foreword

It is with great pleasure that I write the foreword for Five Life Poisons, authored by my long-time student, Deborah Peteler. This book arrives at a time when its message is profoundly needed.

In today's world, while we have achieved incredible material advancements, many of us find ourselves increasingly stressed, dissatisfied, and disconnected from true peace and happiness. The relentless pursuit of material goals often leads to feelings of competition, jealousy, anger, and attachment, creating a cycle of stress and depression. Despite our efforts to find happiness, we unknowingly contribute to our own suffering and unhappiness, as we lose focus on what truly matters—our inner well-being.

Deborah's book provides a timely and practical guide to understanding and addressing the *Five Life Poisons*: anger, ignorance, attachment, ego, and jealousy. These poisons affect all of us. When they arise, we often lose our awareness, become consumed by negativity, and end up causing pain and suffering for ourselves and others. Left unchecked, these poisons lead to frustration, resentment, and an ever-deepening cycle of unhappiness.

What makes this book particularly powerful is its universal appeal and practical approach. Deborah outlines how anyone—whether a spiritual practitioner, a believer, or someone with no specific practice—can use the methods in this book to reflect inward, transform toxic thoughts, and cultivate clarity and positivity. She guides readers through understanding how the poisons arise, and more importantly, how to apply practical techniques to overcome them.

Deborah's insights are not merely theoretical but come from her own deep experience. She has lived these teachings, applying them thoughtfully in her own life. By reflecting, analyzing, and practicing these methods, she has transformed her challenges into tools for growth. Now, she shares this wisdom to benefit others facing similar struggles.

This book provides a clear and compassionate roadmap for healing and transformation. It teaches us to pause, check ourselves, and apply mindful techniques to eliminate negativity and cultivate happiness. By doing so, we can break free from the cycle of suffering and lead brighter, more fulfilling lives.

I wholeheartedly support and commend Deborah for creating this work. Her dedication to this path is evident, and her efforts will undoubtedly benefit countless people. My prayer and wish for readers of this book are that it may guide you to overcome obstacles, find clarity, and live each day with happiness and purpose.

May this book reach many lives and serve as a source of healing, inspiration, and transformation.

With blessings,
Latri Nyima Dakpa Rinpoche

Acknowledgement

Writing The Five Life Poisons has been an incredible journey, and I owe my deepest gratitude to those who have supported, guided, and inspired me along the way.

 To **Latri Nyima Dakpa Rinpoche**, thank you for 27 years of profound teachings and lessons. Your wisdom has been a guiding light in my life, helping me transform my samsaric world for the better. Your guidance has shown me that this work is a constant process, and I am forever grateful for your patience and influence.

 To **my David, David Peteler**, I am so grateful for your unwavering belief in me and for encouraging me to put my thoughts into words. Your role as editor for this book not only helped me but also awakened your own knowledge and understanding of the five poisons. It was truly special for us to come together and collaborate on this project, deepening both our connection and our shared understanding of this transformative work.

To **Nick and Sarah Tichawa of Dream Abbey**, I am immensely grateful for your extra editing, meticulous fact-checking, and enduring friendship. Your support has meant the world to me.

To my children—**Danica, Jason, Justin, Martha, Paili, Edi, Aislynn, Raelyn, Aaron, David, Agness, and Dan**—thank you for your love, patience, and unwavering support. You have been my true inspiration, guiding me to practice wisdom in my everyday life. Your presence has shaped this work more than you will ever know. I hope that I have been an example for you to be fruitful in a positive way, and that the lessons I've learned and shared inspire you in your own lives.

To **Yungdrung Bön**, your teachings over the past 27 years—shared by great Tibetan masters—have gifted me with the tools to help others transform their negativities into wisdom. I am forever grateful for this profound practice and the opportunity to share it with others.

Lastly, to everyone who believed in me and allowed me to pursue my purpose, thank you. This book is a labor of love, wisdom, and gratitude, made possible by each of you.

With all my heart, thank you.

Deborah Peteler

Introduction

Can you relate to any of these feelings?

> *I don't want to be angry all the time, but I just can't help it.*
>
> *My life is filled with a clutter of things and too many toxic relationships. But I can't seem to let them go.*
>
> *I am constantly moody and irritable, and I don't know why.*
>
> *I know what I am doing, and I don't understand why people will not agree with me.*
>
> *I work hard, so why do others have a better life than I do?*

We all have these feelings. They cause unhappiness and suffering in our lives. They take up our time and energy and pull the joy out of life. The key to controlling these emotions is to understand the source of these emotions, how they are triggered, and what we can do to reduce or eliminate them.

The Five Life Poisons

There are many schools of thought and psychological disciplines that seek to understand these feelings and how to deal with them.

Tibetan spirituality identifies "Five Poisons." I like to think of them as the "Five Life Poisons," as they are the basis for so much unhappiness and suffering in our lives.

These Life Poisons are:

> *Ignorance*
>
> *Anger (Aversion)*
>
> *Attachment (Greed, Grasping)*
>
> *Pride*
>
> *Jealousy*

A helpful image to understand these Life Poisons was given to me by a Tibetan Bon monk approximately 27 years ago: Imagine holding onto something, a valuable item. When **Anger** comes into play, we push the object away from us. **Attachment** is when we grasp the object tightly and pull it towards us. **Ignorance** is when we don't even realize we are holding the object. **Pride** or **Ego** is when we stand in a high place and look down on others, thinking we are better than they are. Conversely, **Jealousy** is when we stand in a low place and look up at others, thinking we are not as good as they are.

For the past 27 years, I have had the privilege of studying extensively with my teacher, Latri Nyima Dakpa Rinpoche, along with other Tibetan monks. Through their teachings, I

INTRODUCTION

have gained a profound understanding of these poisons as not merely emotional or mental challenges—they are *Life Poisons* that deeply pervade every aspect of our existence. These toxic forces shape our reactions, relationships, and overall well-being. The knowledge and guidance of the Five Life Poisons from Rinpoche has been truly life-changing for me, offering insights and tools to transform these obstacles into sources of wisdom and healing.

My Introduction to the Five Life Poisons

I was first introduced to the concept of the Five Life Poisons not through formal teachings, but through my upbringing in the church. As a child and young adult, I grew up immersed in sermons and biblical stories that emphasized virtues like kindness and compassion. I remember hearing the story of Cain and Abel, a lesson on the dangers of jealousy. I remember my parents often telling me not to react with anger or envy toward my siblings.

The church also talks about the Seven Deadly Sins, a similar set of negative emotions. These values were familiar, yet they didn't fully resonate with me or change my deeper understanding of myself and the world.

It wasn't until I reached my 30s that my perspective began to shift dramatically. I met a Tibetan Spiritual Master, Latri Nyima Dakpa Rinpoche, a respected senior monk from the Yungdrung Bon tradition. In his teachings, he frequently spoke about the Five Poisons—Anger, Ego, Attachment, Jealousy, and

Ignorance—and how they profoundly influence our well-being, health, and the environments we create. He explained that these poisons shape our negative responses to life, but they don't have to define us. With wisdom, he said, we can change our reactions and transform these poisons into opportunities for growth.

Year after year, I attended Rinpoche's teachings, and gradually, I began to see my life differently. My reactions to anger diminished, and I learned the value of humility. I started to understand the impermanence of life, realizing that our attachment to people, possessions, and ideologies only leads to suffering. I saw jealousy for what it truly is—a destructive force—and found myself learning to feel genuine happiness for others instead of envy. But what truly stayed with me was the concept of ignorance.

In my work as the director and co-founder of AnnapurnaBlue Wellness, I am responsible for conducting wellness retreats. A key element of these wellness retreats is our Mindset Sessions, to help guests make desired changes in their lives. These Mindset Sessions are based on the Five Life Poisons. Through these retreats, I have seen firsthand how this approach has transformed the lives of many guests. Our guests are consistently amazed and empowered by the journey, and we love hearing back from them about their progress. Many share how applying the wisdom of each of the Five Life Poisons has brought improvements across all areas of life: personal, family, relationships, work/career, and finances. This remarkable impact inspired me to write this book and share these teachings

INTRODUCTION

with others, so they too can experience the transformative power of this wisdom.

My hope for this book is to help you understand the significance of each of the Life Poisons. You may find that you're struggling with one, two, three, or even all of the Life Poisons at different times in your life. These can impact everything from your relationships and career to your health and mental well-being.

Sometimes these Five Life Poisons can be easily identified in our daily lives. Sometimes they can subtly and insidiously dominate our emotions and actions without us even realizing it. Being able to recognize and identify these Life Poisons is the first step to reducing their impact on our lives.

According to Tibetan spiritual tradition, for each of the Life Poisons, there is a countermeasure, or wisdom, that can be applied to reduce or remove the Life Poison. These wisdoms are not "quick fixes" or "miracle cures." It takes time and mindful attention to learn the wisdoms and apply them. By learning to recognize the Life Poisons when they arise, and using wisdom to transform them, we can free ourselves from their negative effects, bring our daily lives more in our own control, and find balance and live a more peaceful, fulfilling life.

Bringing Freedom, Balance and Healing

By recognizing that each Life Poison has an antidote, we open the door to transformation. When the Life Poisons arise—and they inevitably will—we have the power to pause, reflect, and choose how to respond. Will we respond with our negative emotions, based on old internal patterns? Or will we respond with wisdom? Over time, these antidotes become natural responses. They allows us to free ourselves from the "knee jerk reflex" emotional reactions and make better life decisions. They also help us cultivate inner balance, heal emotional wounds, and create more harmonious relationships.

The journey of applying these antidotes isn't about eliminating emotions, but about transforming our relationship with them. Instead of letting anger, jealousy, or attachment control us, we can choose patience, gratitude, and acceptance to guide us. This process leads to personal growth, emotional healing, and a more peaceful, empowered way of living.

By understanding the Five Life Poisons and embracing the wisdoms, we restore balance to our life, nurturing our mind, body, and spirit, and ultimately, fostering a deeper connection with ourselves and others.

Ready to Start Your Journey? Some Useful Tools.

Focus. Find a comfortable place to focus on and absorb this book's wisdom and embark on your journey.

Journal. Journaling is a great tool for collecting your thoughts and tracking your progress. I have found that it's best to have a separate journal for this journey.

Cultivate Awareness. To recognize and understand the Life Poisons requires a high degree of self-awareness. A good way to develop self-awareness is through practicing mindfulness and compassion.

Practice Mindfulness. Mindfulness is the practice of fully embracing the present moment, with a heart open to curiosity and free of judgment. It invites us to engage wholeheartedly in whatever we are doing—whether it's as simple as eating a meal, taking a walk, or even breathing—without letting our minds wander to worries about the future or regrets of the past. At its essence, mindfulness is about being here, now, and being aware of our thoughts, feelings, and sensations without letting them dictate our reactions. This allows us to observe rather than be consumed by our inner experiences, giving us a powerful tool to navigate life with more ease and clarity.

As I've experienced through my own practice and studies, mindfulness offers profound benefits that ripple into every part of life. One of the greatest gifts of mindfulness is its ability to reduce stress and anxiety.[i] By grounding us in the present, mindfulness disrupts the relentless cycles of worry that can take over our minds, helping us feel a greater sense of calm and balance. This sense of calm extends into our emotional lives as well, where mindfulness can help us respond to emotions thoughtfully rather than impulsively. Over time, we find ourselves feeling more resilient and prepared to handle whatever challenges arise.

Mindfulness also has the wonderful side effect of sharpening our focus and concentration, which can enhance our productivity and help us stay fully engaged with our tasks.[ii] In a world filled with constant distractions, this ability to bring our attention back to the present moment becomes invaluable. Not only does it improve our mental clarity, but it can also benefit our physical health. Research shows that mindfulness can positively affect the body, from lowering blood pressure and boosting the immune system to helping us manage pain and reduce the effects of chronic stress.[iii] When we connect our minds and bodies in this way, we open the door to a greater level of well-being.

Mindfulness gives us the gift of self-awareness. It allows us to notice our habitual thought patterns, helping us see ourselves more clearly and, in time, accept ourselves more fully. This self-awareness fosters personal growth, compassion, and even a deeper sense of purpose.

As we learn to understand and accept ourselves, we also begin to cultivate empathy and compassion for others. Mindfulness nurtures our ability to listen and connect, enriching our relationships and expanding our capacity for kindness.

Incorporating mindfulness into daily life isn't about escaping reality; rather, it's about learning to fully engage with it. By embracing this practice, we create a foundation for navigating life's inevitable ups and downs with grace and resilience. Mindfulness helps us live more authentically, compassionately, and intentionally. And in this mindful presence, we often find a profound peace—a peace that stems not from having a perfect life but from meeting life as it is, moment by moment, with open arms.

INTRODUCTION

Sarah was a caring mother and wife who juggled many responsibilities. Every day, she woke up early to prepare breakfast, get her children ready for school, and rush off to her job at a local office. From the moment she opened her eyes, her mind was already in overdrive, planning, organizing, and mentally ticking off the tasks that awaited her. She was always on the go, and although she loved her family, friends, and career, she often felt as if life was speeding past her.

One evening, after a long day at work, Sarah's youngest daughter, Emma, tugged at her sleeve, asking her to read a story before bed. Exhausted, and her mind filled with tomorrow's agenda, Sarah sighed and gave Emma a quick hug, promising to read to her "another night." Emma looked disappointed, but Sarah was already thinking about the work emails she still had to check and the lunches she needed to pack. She didn't notice the way Emma's shoulders slumped as she walked to her room.

As the weeks went on, Sarah's life became even busier. She found herself saying "not now" or "maybe later" more often than she'd like to admit. She missed school recitals and family dinners, always telling herself she would make it up to them when things calmed down. But days turned into months, and Sarah's days remained a blur of tasks and responsibilities. She missed small moments, like her husband's stories from work or the laughter of her children at play. She was always there physically, but her mind was elsewhere, anticipating the next chore or planning the next day.

One evening, Sarah received a letter from her daughter's teacher, inviting parents to a class event where each child would read a short letter they had written about someone they admired. Sarah, for once, made time to attend, feeling proud as she imagined Emma's letter.

When Emma stood to read, her small voice trembled a bit. "The person I admire is my mom," she began. Sarah smiled, her heart swelling with pride. But as Emma continued, Sarah felt a lump form in her throat. "My mom is really busy, and I know she loves me," Emma read. "Sometimes she doesn't have time to play or read stories, but I hope one day we can do those things together, maybe when she has more time."

Sarah felt her heart sink. She realized then, as she looked around the room at other smiling parents and family members, how much she had missed. In her constant busyness and unawareness, she had overlooked small but meaningful moments to truly connect to her loved ones. Emma's simple words made her see the gap between her intentions and her actions.

That night, Sarah sat down and reflected on the choices she had been making. She realized that she had been so focused on checking off boxes and completing tasks that she had forgotten to truly be present. Her busyness had distracted her from what mattered most—connecting with her family, enjoying moments of joy, and simply being there for the people she loved.

With this realization, Sarah decided to make a change. She began practicing mindfulness in small ways—taking a few deep breaths in the morning before she started her day, giving her full attention to her children when they spoke, and letting go of the need to constantly rush from one task to the next. She learned to pause,

INTRODUCTION

to listen, and to appreciate the little moments she had previously missed.

In time, Sarah noticed a transformation in her relationships. Her children opened up more, eager to share their stories with her, and she found herself genuinely enjoying their laughter and play. Her husband, too, felt closer to her as they shared quiet moments together, no longer overshadowed by Sarah's constant planning and thinking.

Sarah learned that mindfulness was not about ignoring her responsibilities but about being fully present for each task and each person. By letting go of the endless mental checklist, she discovered a newfound sense of peace and connection. She realized that life wasn't something to be rushed through but to be fully experienced. And as she embraced mindfulness, she felt, for the first time in years, that she was truly living, connected deeply to herself and the people she loved.

Sarah's experience shows how easy it is to slip into "doing" mode and miss the moments that truly matter. Her shift toward mindful presence reminds us that life unfolds most vibrantly when we pause, breathe, and truly connect—both with ourselves and others.

Compassion: The Universal Antidote for Negativity

Compassion is the act of opening our hearts to others and to ourselves, allowing us to connect with kindness, understanding, and a desire to ease suffering. At its core, compassion is the willingness to see another's pain and to respond with warmth and empathy. It's a courageous choice to extend ourselves, often asking us to set aside judgments and meet others—and even our own struggles—with grace and caring.

One of the profound benefits of compassion is that it doesn't just uplift those we care for; it also transforms us in unexpected ways. When we respond to others with compassion, we strengthen our own resilience and deepen our capacity for patience and understanding. Compassion broadens our perspective, helping us move beyond self-centered concerns and connect on a deeper level. In this way, compassion can make us feel more rooted, more engaged with the world around us, and ultimately, more fulfilled.

What's important to remember about compassion is that it is by no means a sign of weakness. Compassion requires inner strength; it asks us to remain open even when faced with hardship or discomfort. In many ways, compassion is a form of courage, the courage to see beyond someone's actions or words, beyond our own frustrations, and to recognize humanity in each situation. When we show compassion, we create a safe space for healing, for forgiveness, and for understanding.

For example, when we approach a challenging situation with compassion, whether in a relationship, a work setting, or even with a stranger, we often find that our response shifts the energy around us. Our compassionate presence can diffuse tension, break down barriers, and inspire others to feel seen and valued. And sometimes, this simple shift in perspective, the willingness to show kindness rather than judgment—can open the door to a

INTRODUCTION

meaningful connection or a deeper understanding of one another.

Compassion, then, is not just a gift we give others; it's a gift we give ourselves. It helps us release anger, frustration, and judgment, and fills us with a sense of peace, connection, and purpose. In embracing compassion, we discover that kindness and understanding are not signs of weakness but the foundation of a powerful, transformative strength.

These key points and tools will serve as your compass, helping you identify, navigate and transform the obstacles and negativities in your life.

Disclaimer

This book was written to help readers understand the Five Life Poisons and the profound effects these emotional forces can have on our lives. It provides insights and practical tools for recognizing, managing, and transforming these poisons.

However, personal growth and self-reflection can sometimes bring up deeper emotions and unresolved experiences.

If you find yourself experiencing intense emotional distress, past trauma resurfacing, or overwhelming feelings, please seek professional support from a licensed therapist, counselor, or mental health professional. You do not have to navigate this journey alone—help is available.

This book is a guide for transformation, but true healing is a process, and sometimes additional support is necessary. Your well-being is important.

1

Anger

Anger is when we push the object away from us.

Phil was known for his short fuse. He had a knack for blowing up over the smallest things, from spilled coffee to squeaky doors. His friends joked that he was like a firecracker ready to pop, but Phil didn't mind—he prided himself on being "direct" and "passionate."

One Saturday morning, Phil decided to build a birdhouse. Armed with a hammer, nails, and a plan, he set to work in his backyard, determined to make it perfect. But as soon as he began, things went south. He missed a nail and hammered his thumb instead. Furious, he threw the hammer across the yard, only to have it land in his prized tomato plants.

"That's it!" he shouted. "This birdhouse is cursed!"

Phil stormed inside, but his anger followed him. Later, his neighbor came over, asking if everything was okay. "You wouldn't understand," Phil grumbled, still fuming. "This stupid birdhouse ruined my tomatoes!" The neighbor couldn't help but laugh, replying, "Phil, it wasn't the birdhouse. It was your temper that did the damage!"

Phil paused, realizing the truth in his words, but not quite ready to admit it. Determined to calm down, he took a deep breath and went back to his project with a new approach. This time, he stayed focused and tried not to let little things get to him. Sure enough, he managed to finish the birdhouse—though a bit crooked—and found himself laughing at the whole ordeal.

From that day on, Phil tried a different approach with his anger, realizing it was more fun to laugh than to rage. His tomato plants never suffered another "attack," and his friends noticed he was a lot more relaxed—even if his birdhouses still leaned a bit to the left!

The first Life Poison is generally known as Anger. We can use other related terms such as hatred, aversion, and avoidance. Anger is like when we hold an object or person and push it away from ourselves, usually with a high degree of attached emotion.

Phil's outburst highlights how anger can spiral when left unchecked. Recognizing that moment of rage allowed him to pause and approach the situation with a calmer mind. His story reminds us that identifying anger early is the first step toward transforming it into clarity and healthier communication.

Sometimes, anger can be a response to underlying frustrations, feeling misunderstood, or unmet expectations. This anger might become a cycle if left unaddressed, showing up as general irritability and moodiness.

Anger is often described as a fire—a sudden, intense, and consuming emotion that can burn everything in its path. It's one of the most powerful of the Five Life Poisons because it can easily take control of us, affecting not only our mental and emotional well-being but also our physical health and the people around us. When anger arises, it clouds our ability to see clearly, distorts our judgment, and often leads us to react in ways that we later regret. Understanding the nature of anger, how it manifests, and the wisdom that can transform it is crucial for finding inner peace and balance.

The Emotions of Anger: The Fire Within

Anger can take many forms—frustration, irritation, resentment, or rage. It often arises when we feel threatened, disrespected, or hurt, whether by a person, a situation, or even ourselves. The intensity of anger can range from a mild annoyance to a full-blown outburst of rage, but the underlying emotion is always a response to some form of perceived injustice or unmet need.

When anger is triggered, our body responds almost immediately: our heart rate increases, our muscles tense, and we may feel a rush of heat. Emotionally, we feel a sense of power—like we're ready to fight or defend ourselves. In the heat of the moment, anger can feel justified, even righteous. But this sense of power is fleeting and often leads to destructive outcomes. Instead of resolving the situation, anger escalates it, leaving us and those around us hurt or disconnected.

The emotional toll of anger doesn't stop when the moment passes. It lingers, feeding on itself, and can create a cycle where frustration builds, leading to more frequent outbursts. When left unchecked, anger becomes a habitual response to stress or challenges, reinforcing negative patterns in our lives.

How Anger Affects Us and Those Around Us

Anger doesn't exist in isolation—it ripples outward, affecting everyone in its path. Anger can change how we interact with the world, making us reactive rather than thoughtful. It distorts our view of situations, causing us to see threats or injustice where there may be none. This distortion often leads to impulsive decisions that aren't based on reason or clarity but on the intensity of the emotion.

In relationships, anger pushes people away. Whether it's between partners, family members, friends, or colleagues, the outbursts, harsh words, and conflicts that arise from anger create a divide. Trust is eroded, and people begin to distance themselves, not knowing when another outburst might occur. Over time, this can leave the angry person feeling isolated and unsupported, even though what they may truly need is connection and understanding.

This emotion is particularly damaging in our personal and professional lives. Anger creates barriers to effective communication and collaboration. In a work setting, it can damage our reputation, hinder productivity, and block opportunities for growth. People may start avoiding difficult conversations with us, or they may hesitate to share ideas or collaborate out of fear of triggering our anger. In personal relationships, the constant tension caused by anger can lead to breakdowns in communication, unresolved conflicts, and emotional distance.

The Health Consequences of Anger

Anger is not just an emotional storm; it can also place our physical health at risk. When we feel anger rising, our body activates the fight-or-flight response, sending stress hormones like cortisol and adrenaline coursing through our system.[iv] A short burst of these hormones can be helpful in true emergencies, but chronic or frequent anger means our body remains in this heightened state day after day.

The body's reaction to anger, including the release of stress hormones like cortisol, can also disrupt the digestive system, leading to issues like stomachaches, acid reflux, and even long-term gastrointestinal problems.[v]

Over time, that constant strain and stress can lead to high blood pressure and a greater risk of heart disease or stroke.[vi] Anger can also weaken our immune system, making us more prone to illnesses and slowing our recovery.[vii]

Because anger tends to linger in our thoughts, it often contributes to anxiety, depression, and disrupted sleep.[viii] Without adequate rest, it becomes even harder to regulate our emotions, creating a vicious cycle where anger feeds into more anger. By recognizing and managing anger before it takes over, we can help protect both our mental balance and our long-term health.

Transforming Anger: Pausing and The Wisdom of Compassion

The good news is that anger, like all Life Poisons, can be transformed through wisdom. The antidotes to anger are **pausing** and **compassion**—wisdoms that calm the fire and allow us to respond to life's challenges with grace and clarity instead of reactivity.

We need to develop the ability to pause, to take a step back and allow the intensity of emotion to pass before responding. It is recognizing that anger is often a temporary surge of emotion, and that if we give ourselves time to breathe and reflect, we can regain control of the situation. Patience teaches us to be less reactive and more thoughtful. When anger arises, take a moment to ask yourself: *Is this reaction helpful? Will it resolve the situation, or make it worse?* Simply by giving yourself this pause, you create space for a wiser response.

Compassion doesn't mean ignoring our feelings; it means addressing them with kindness and understanding rather than aggression.

Compassion allows us to understand the pain or frustration behind anger, both in ourselves and in others. It invites us to look at the situation with empathy rather than judgment. When we feel anger rising, try to shift your perspective: *What is really causing this anger? Is it fear, disappointment, or hurt? Is it something else?*

By looking deeper, we can begin to dissolve the anger and replace it with compassion for ourselves and others involved.

Practices to Calm the Beast of Anger

There are practical steps you can take to apply the wisdom of pausing and compassion to calm the fire of anger before it consumes you. These practices not only help to manage anger in the moment but also contribute to creating a more positive response and outcome for yourself in both your personal and professional life.

Breathwork: When you feel anger rising, focus on your breath. Take slow, deep breaths, inhaling through the nose and exhaling through the mouth. This simple practice helps calm your nervous system and gives you the space to regain control of your emotions.

Mindfulness: Mindfulness meditation is an effective way to recognize when anger is building within you. When you begin to feel emotions rising, stop and ask yourself, "What is this feeling? Where is it coming from? How can I redirect it?" By cultivating awareness of your thoughts and feelings, you can catch the early signs of anger and make a conscious choice not to let it escalate.

Pause and Reflect Before Reacting: Make a habit to pause before responding when you're angry. Give yourself a moment to consider the consequences of your words or actions. Will they bring resolution, or will they fuel the fire? This pause helps you respond with clarity and aids in a more positive outcome.

Journaling: Writing about your anger can help you process it without taking it out on others. By putting your feelings into words, you can gain clarity about what's really bothering you and how you want to address it.

Here is a prompt to get started. Think back to a recent moment when anger flared up. Ask yourself:

- Why was I angry?
- What was the real trigger: a situation, a past hurt, or my own expectations?
- How did it feel in my body? Tension? Heat? A rush of energy?
- If I could go back, what would I do differently?

Use these reflections to pinpoint the root of your anger and explore how you might pause or redirect that energy next time.

Physical Release: Anger creates energy in the body that needs to be released. Try channeling this energy into physical activities like exercise, yoga, or taking a walk. This can help release the tension while giving your mind time to cool down.

Transforming Anger with Pausing and Compassion

Anger is a powerful force, but it doesn't have to control us. By recognizing when anger arises, stepping back, and applying the wisdom of patience and compassion, we can transform this Life

Poison into a force for growth and understanding. Each time we choose to respond with wisdom instead of reactivity, we weaken the grip of anger and create more space for peace, balance, and positive outcomes in our life.

In both personal and professional life, learning to control our anger and not react impulsively leads to better, more positive outcomes. We'll notice improved communication, stronger relationships, and greater success when we choose wisdom over reaction. Anger will continue to arise from time to time, but with wisdom, we can calm the beast and make choices that lead to a more harmonious and fulfilling life.

2

Attachment

Attachment is when we grasp an object tightly and pull it towards us.

In a bustling city, a woman named Mira was known for her determination to control every aspect of her life. She believed that with enough effort, she could shape her perfect world—a beautiful home, a thriving career, and a stable, flawless routine. Her desire for control gave her a sense of security, as if she could protect herself from the uncertainties of life. But deep down, she feared change, clinging to the illusion that everything she built could last forever.

As the years passed, Mira's attachment to control became an invisible burden. The pressure to keep things exactly as she wanted drained her energy, leaving her anxious, sleepless, and constantly on edge. Whenever things didn't go her way—a project failed, or a friend drifted apart—she felt as though her world was collapsing. The illusion of permanence she held onto left her feeling unsteady and exhausted.

One day, a sudden storm hit the city, flooding streets and uprooting trees. Mira's home, her sanctuary, was damaged beyond recognition. Shocked and heartbroken, she wandered aimlessly, feeling as if she had lost herself in the chaos.

A gentle stranger, seeing her despair, offered a simple truth: "Life is like the sea—always moving, always changing." Mira stopped for a moment. Suddenly, she realized that clinging to the illusion of permanence only makes the storms harder to bear. True peace lies in acceptance, letting go of the need to control, and embracing the flow of life.

Mira's struggle illustrates the burden that attachment can place on our lives—and how letting go can create space for true peace.

Attachment, one of the most deeply rooted of the Five Life Poisons, can be a powerful force that creates significant suffering when we cling too tightly to people, possessions, ideas, or outcomes. At its core, attachment is the desire to hold on to something or someone because we believe it will bring us happiness, security, or fulfillment.

But this idea that attachment brings happiness is false. By grasping onto things—whether material things, illusions of control, relationships, or a desire to keep everything the same and not let it change—we bind ourselves to expectations that are often beyond our control. This leads to disappointment, anxiety, and a sense of loss when the impermanence of life inevitably brings change. Often, when we become disappointed with grasping one thing, we move on to grasp something else instead, in a vain hope that more grasping will make us happy.

Understanding how attachment manifests, how it affects our well-being, and the wisdom that can help release this toxic emotion is key to cultivating a healthier and more balanced life.

The Emotions of Attachment: The Chains That Bind

Attachment can evoke a wide range of emotions, from desire and hope to anxiety, fear, and grief. On the surface, attachment often feels like love or loyalty, but when examined more closely, it becomes clear that the emotion is rooted in clinging, control, and dependency.

When we are attached to something—whether it's a relationship, a material possession, or a particular outcome—our emotions become dependent on whether we can maintain that attachment. The mere thought of losing what we hold dear can evoke fear, insecurity, and anxiety. In many cases, attachment arises from a desire for control. We want things to stay the way we like them, and we struggle to accept that life is constantly changing. This need for control often leads to stress and frustration when reality doesn't align with our expectations.

For example, we might feel deeply attached to a relationship, believing that our happiness depends on the other person staying in our life. While it's natural to care about others, when attachment becomes excessive, it turns into a fear of losing that connection. This fear often results in clinginess, jealousy, or emotional manipulation—behaviors that can ultimately push others away.

The emotions of attachment also extend beyond relationships. People often become attached to material possessions, status, or even ideas about who they think they should be. This leads to feelings of dissatisfaction, as the attachment to something external prevents them from finding peace within themselves.

How Attachment Affects Us and Those Around Us

The effects of attachment go beyond our internal emotional state; they ripple outward, affecting the people in our lives and the ways we interact with the world. When we're attached to someone or something, we create a mental dependency that often leads to unhealthy behaviors and strained relationships.

In personal relationships, attachment can cause possessiveness, jealousy, or a fear of abandonment. These emotions stem from the belief that our happiness or sense of self is tied to another person's actions or presence. As a result, we may place unfair expectations on others, leading to conflict and emotional imbalance. For example, if we're overly attached to a partner, we may fear losing them to the point where we try to control their actions or become overly demanding of their time and attention. This creates tension and drives a wedge between us and the other person, as they may feel suffocated or unable to meet our expectations.

Attachment also affects our relationship with the material world. When we become attached to possessions, status, or a specific outcome, we may experience stress and anxiety from fear of losing these things. We might work excessively to maintain a certain lifestyle or push ourselves toward a goal at the expense of our well-being, all because we believe that our worth or happiness is tied to these external markers of success. In doing so, we lose sight of what truly matters—our inner peace and well-being.

Moreover, attachment can limit our personal growth. When we cling to ideas about who we are or what we should achieve, we close ourselves off to new opportunities and perspectives. This creates a fixed mindset, where any deviation from our expectations feels like a failure rather than a chance to evolve.

The Health Consequences of Attachment

Just as anger can place us on high alert, attachment creates its own form of sustained stress rooted in our fear of losing something (or someone). Unlike anger's more explosive nature, attachment exerts a quieter but persistent pressure. When we cling to relationships, possessions, or outcomes, our body often interprets this anxiety as a threat, flooding us with cortisol over long stretches of time.

As a result, our immune system weakens, and blood pressure can remain elevated, increasing our vulnerability to conditions like heart disease.[ix] Constantly worrying about maintaining or protecting what we have can also deplete our emotional energy, leading to feelings of burnout or disengagement.

On top of that, attachment fosters insecurity, leaving us anxious or restless if we sense any risk to what we hold dear. This mental strain frequently keeps us awake at night, compromising our sleep and amplifying the next day's stress.

By noticing these attachment-driven tensions and learning to let go, we create space for healthier emotional and physical well-being.

The Root Causes of Attachment

To understand how attachment operates in our lives, it's important to explore the root causes that fuel it.

At the core of attachment is often a deep-seated fear of losing something that we believe is essential for our happiness or security. This fear drives us to hold on tightly, leading to anxiety and emotional dependency.

Attachment is also rooted in the desire for control. We often want things to go a certain way, to stay the same, or to meet our expectations. We develop a sense of dependency on external factors to keep our illusions or expectations. This leads to disappointment when things inevitably change.

Many people identify with external objects. They attach their self-worth to possessions, relationships, or achievements, believing that these external things define them. When these attachments are threatened, it feels like a personal loss of identity.

Attachment also often stems from the belief that things are permanent, leading to a resistance to change and suffering when the inevitable happens. This illusion of permanence further increases both our attachment and the suffering that it causes.

Finally, when we lack inner fulfillment—when we feel incomplete within ourselves—we often seek fulfillment through external attachments, hoping they will fill the void. But this external seeking never truly satisfies the deeper need for inner peace.

Transforming Attachment: The Wisdom of Non-Attachment and Acceptance

The antidote to attachment is **non-attachment** and **acceptance**—the wisdom that teaches us to let go of the need to control outcomes and release emotional dependency on external things. This doesn't mean that we stop caring about people or lose interest in life's joys, but rather that we learn to experience life without clinging to it. Non-attachment allows us to enjoy the present moment without the constant fear of loss.

Non-attachment doesn't mean disengagement or indifference; it means recognizing that everything in life is impermanent. Relationships, material possessions, and life circumstances are constantly changing. Clinging to them only leads to suffering. By practicing non-attachment, we learn to appreciate what we have in the moment while letting go of the need to control its outcome. This wisdom frees us from the emotional rollercoaster of attachment and allows us to experience life with greater peace.

Acceptance is the wisdom that teaches us to embrace life as it is—not as we wish it to be. It is the understanding that change is a natural part of life, and that resisting inevitable change only leads to pain. By accepting that we cannot control everything, we open ourselves up to the flow of life, allowing us to move through challenges and transitions with grace. Acceptance helps dissolve the fear and anxiety that attachment creates, allowing us to live more fully in the present moment.

Practices to Release the Grip of Attachment

Releasing attachment is a process that requires conscious effort and practice. Here are some steps to help you cultivate non-attachment and acceptance in your life:

Impermanence: The only constant in the world is change. This understanding of impermanence is the quiet reminder that life, in all its forms, is constantly in motion.

Practice observing a beautiful flower. Focus on what makes it beautiful—its color, shape, and fragrance. Then, think about how the flower will age, wilt and droop, change color, and ultimately die.

Now think about a friendship. At one point, you didn't know your friend. Then, you met, and you developed the friendship. Over time, you will both experience challenges and changes. Both you and the person who is a close friend today will change. You may cease to be friends. You may drift away, or you may in fact come to dislike each other. Think about how this has happened in your life and can happen again.

Japanese culture provides an interesting example of embracing impermanence. In early April, people in Japan celebrate "cherry blossom time." There are three stages of the cherry blossoms. The first is when the blossoms are freshly opened and sweet-smelling. The second is when they mature and begin to fade. The third is when the blossoms wilt, discolor and begin to fall. It is said that everyone likes the first stage of the new, fresh blossoms. Some can also appreciate the change and beauty of the second stage. But only one who truly understands life can also see the beauty of the third stage and embrace its message of impermanence.

Like waves that rise and fall in the ocean, every experience, relationship, and moment ebbs and flows, never to remain the same. Embracing impermanence allows us to appreciate each moment for what it is, free from the fear of losing it. In acceptance, we find a deep peace, realizing that the beauty of life lies not in its permanence, but in its ever-changing nature.

Mindfulness Meditation: We have already discussed mindfulness and will continue to raise this key tool for recognizing and overcoming the Life Poisons. Mindfulness meditation is a powerful practice for observing your thoughts and emotions without becoming attached to them. As you meditate, notice when feelings of attachment arise—whether it's a desire to hold onto something or a fear of losing it. Think to yourself, "there was a time for that, but that time has passed," and release it. By observing these thoughts without judgment, you can begin to release their hold on you.

Letting Go Rituals: Engage in small letting go rituals to practice non-attachment. For example, decluttering your living space can be a symbolic way of releasing your attachment to material possessions. As you let go of items, remind yourself that your happiness and worth are not tied to things.

Gratitude Practice: Cultivating gratitude helps you shift your focus from what you fear losing to what you have in the present. By practicing gratitude, you train your mind to appreciate life as it is, rather than constantly striving for more or fearing loss.

Self-Reflection: Reflect on areas of your life where attachment is causing stress or suffering. Ask yourself: *What am I clinging to? Why do I feel the need to hold on so tightly?* By gaining clarity about the roots of your attachment, you can begin to release it.

Journaling: Recall a time when you found it difficult to let go—perhaps of a possession, a person, or simply the idea that something had to go "your way." Consider:

- What made this so hard to release?
- Was I fearing loss, craving control, or confusing my self-worth with that external thing?
- Once I released it, how did I feel?
- In hindsight, did clinging to it bring me more peace or more worry?

Write about your experience to see if there are any patterns that keep you holding on too tightly.

Transforming Attachment With Non-Attachment

Attachment, while a natural human tendency, can become a source of significant suffering when it binds us to things, people, or outcomes that are beyond our control. The emotions of attachment—fear, anxiety, and insecurity—keep us stuck in a cycle of clinging and disappointment. But by cultivating the wisdom of non-attachment and acceptance, we can begin to release the hold that attachment has on us and our lives.

Non-attachment allows us to experience life more freely, enjoying what we have without the constant fear of losing it. Acceptance teaches us to flow with life's changes, embracing the impermanence of all things. By practicing these wisdoms, we will find that we are more at peace, less reactive to external circumstances, and able to cultivate deeper, healthier relationships with ourselves and others.

Releasing attachment doesn't mean we stop caring—it means we care with an open heart, free from the chains of dependency. With time and practice, we will discover that non-attachment is not about losing anything, but about gaining true freedom and inner peace.

3

Ignorance

Ignorance is when we don't even realize we're holding the object.

In a bustling city, there lived a man named Tom who thought he knew everything he needed to navigate life. Successful in his career and confident in his views, he dismissed the need for advice, convinced that his way was the best way. Tom rarely bothered with perspectives different from his own, scrolling past articles that challenged his beliefs and cutting off conversations that questioned his choices. This self-assured ignorance seeped into all aspects of his life.

As time went on, Tom began facing unexpected problems. His once-thriving career started to stall as he overlooked new trends, believing his old methods would always work. His health began to decline, but he ignored it, insisting he didn't need doctors or lifestyle changes. His relationships grew strained as friends and family pulled away, frustrated by his refusal to listen or empathize. Isolated and increasingly anxious, Tom couldn't understand why his world seemed to be unraveling.

One evening, while alone in a café, Tom overheard an elderly woman sharing advice with a friend, saying, "Wisdom isn't about knowing everything; it's about knowing when you don't know and being open to learn and understand."

Tom's unraveling world shows how assumptions and a rigid worldview can backfire when reality crashes in. By stumbling on the simple insight that "wisdom is knowing when you don't know," Tom began to open up to new perspectives. His experience reveals that acknowledging our own limitations and questions is a key step in dissolving the Life Poison of Ignorance.

Ignorance, one of the most subtle and pervasive of the Five Life Poisons, silently impacts every area of our life. While often misunderstood as merely "not knowing," ignorance goes much deeper than just a lack of information. It is a state of being unaware of the truth of a situation, ourselves, or the world around us. Ignorance is not realizing that we are pushing things away or pulling things towards us; we don't even realize we're holding on at all. This lack of awareness prevents us from seeing things as they truly are, leading us to make decisions based on false assumptions, limited perspectives, and incomplete understandings. It clouds our judgment, narrows our vision, and hinders personal and spiritual growth. Understanding how ignorance manifests, how it affects our lives, and the wisdom that can transform it is essential for cultivating a more enlightened, balanced way of living.

Ignorance is a deep-rooted poison, fueled by factors such as our culture, our upbringing, lack of self-awareness, fear of the unknown, and the ego's resistance to admitting mistakes. Sometimes we refer to our ignorance as a "blind spot." This is a helpful term, as it suggests we simply can't see a problem, rather than assigning blame or negativity. To transform ignorance into wisdom, we must first recognize its root causes—our fear, conditioning, and avoidance. Once we cultivate mindfulness, curiosity, and humility, ignorance can give way to greater understanding, clarity, and growth.

The Emotions of Ignorance: The Fog of Confusion

Ignorance can be compared to a fog—obscuring the truth, keeping us in the dark, and limiting our ability to navigate the complexities of life. When we operate from a place of ignorance, emotions such as anger, attachment, confusion, frustration, and even fear tend to dominate. Often, we don't realize we're acting from ignorance because it feels familiar, even comfortable, to rely on the limited knowledge or perspective we have. However, this false sense of security can lead to misguided beliefs and assumptions.

For example, we might feel certain that a colleague or friend has wronged us, acting on our immediate perceptions without considering their side of the story. This emotional response, born from ignorance, can escalate conflict unnecessarily. The frustration that follows often makes situations worse because we fail to consider the bigger picture or acknowledge the limitations of our own understanding.

Ignorance also feeds into other negative emotions such as defensiveness and stubbornness. When we don't fully understand something, we may feel insecure, leading us to cling to our beliefs even more tightly. This stubbornness becomes a way of protecting ourselves from the fear of being wrong or vulnerable, causing us to push away new ideas, perspectives, or opportunities for growth. This vicious circle stops our growth and moves us deeper into the problem.

What Causes Ignorance?

Ignorance doesn't simply happen—it has roots in various internal and external factors that shape how we see the world. It often stems from a lack of self-awareness—not fully understanding our own thoughts, emotions, or motivations. Without self-awareness, we remain disconnected from the deeper truths of why we react the way we do, leading to confusion in decision-making.

From childhood, we are conditioned by societal norms, family values, and cultural beliefs. These ingrained patterns can limit our perspective, preventing us from questioning or challenging the assumptions we've inherited. As we age, we may start to realize that fear, especially of the unknown, plays a significant role in ignorance. We tend to avoid what we don't understand, fearing that new perspectives or information might threaten our worldview or sense of security. When we lose our curiosity about life and stop seeking new knowledge or understanding, ignorance settles in. The desire to explore different perspectives and ideas is key to overcoming ignorance.

Ego-driven ignorance and pride causes us to hold tightly to our beliefs, making us reluctant to admit we don't know something or that we might be wrong. Our need to protect our self-image can prevent growth.

In a world filled with constant distractions and demands on our attention, we can easily fall into surface-level thinking. This lack of reflection leads to automatic reactions based on old habits, not mindful awareness.

Some people avoid confronting emotions, especially the more uncomfortable ones, choosing instead to remain ignorant of the deeper issues that drive their behavior. This avoidance perpetuates ignorance and prevents healing or transformation.

How Ignorance Affects Us and Those Around Us

Operating from a place of ignorance affects not just our internal state but also how we interact with the world. It distorts our relationships, creates unnecessary conflict, and prevents us from seeing the deeper truth in any situation. When ignorance governs our thoughts and actions, we're less likely to listen to others, less open to learning, and more prone to jump to conclusions. This can lead to misunderstandings, damaged relationships, and missed opportunities. For example, a friend or partner may express a concern or criticism. Instead of taking time to understand where they're coming from, we might react defensively, assuming they're attacking us. This reaction, rooted in ignorance and old reflexive patterns, prevents deeper communication and trust from forming. Over time, this pattern pushes people away, as they feel unheard, misunderstood, or dismissed.

Ignorance can also limit our personal and professional growth. In the workplace, we might resist feedback or dismiss new ideas because they challenge our current understanding. This not only stunts our development but also creates an environment where others may feel hesitant to engage or collaborate with us because of our negativity. It can lead to stagnation and even cause us to fall behind in our career, as we're unwilling to see beyond our existing knowledge or perspective, often alienating our colleagues in the process.

The Health Consequences of Ignorance

Anger and attachment highlight two different stress responses, but ignorance—living with incomplete knowledge or refusing to see beyond our own assumptions—introduces a different kind of strain. When we operate on false or limited understanding, we stay caught in cycles of confusion, frustration, and worry about the unknown. Our body perceives this perpetual uncertainty as another type of threat, which also elevates cortisol levels and keeps us on edge.[x]

Because ignorance can leave us feeling powerless or fearful, it also drains our mental energy. We may find ourselves mentally exhausted by trying to piece together partial information or by avoiding details that make us uncomfortable.

Over time, chronic stress of this kind can weaken our immune system and increase our risk of heart disease, much like other Life Poisons. Additionally, with increased stress, poor sleep often follows, as our unsettled mind replays misunderstandings or unanswered questions.

Ignorance isn't just an abstract concept—it takes a real toll on our mind and body. By using the antidotes, we can prevent ignorance from quietly undercutting our physical and emotional health.

Transforming Ignorance: The Wisdom of Awareness and Openness

The antidote to ignorance is **awareness** and **openness**, the wisdom that encourages us to step back, learn more, and see all sides of a situation before reacting. Developing awareness means cultivating the ability to recognize when our understanding is limited. When we can recognize this, it allows us to be open to learning more, whether it's about ourselves, others, or the world around us.

Awareness is about recognizing when ignorance is at play—when we don't know the full story or when our perspective may be limited. It's the humility to acknowledge that our view is not the only one, and that others may have insights or information that we don't.

The key to cultivating awareness is mindfulness. As we work to transform the Life Poison of Ignorance, we continue going deeper into our mindfulness practice. Through this, we can notice when we're reacting impulsively based on assumptions rather than facts. Our mindfulness helps us pause, reflect, and ask ourselves: *What don't I know here? What am I not seeing?*

Openness to learning means being willing to seek out knowledge, listen to others, and expand our understanding. Instead of reacting to a situation from a place of ignorance, openness invites us to explore multiple sides of an issue. When faced with a challenge or conflict, ask questions instead of jumping to conclusions. Take time to understand different perspectives and be open to new insights. This openness is essential for transforming ignorance into wisdom.

Practices to Transform Ignorance into Wisdom

Here are some practical steps to cultivate awareness and openness and break free from the cycle of ignorance.

Pause and Reflect: Before reacting to a situation, take a moment to pause and reflect. Ask: *Do I really understand what's going on here? Am I missing information?* This simple pause can help prevent you from acting on incomplete knowledge and encourage you to seek more clarity.

Mindful Listening: Practice mindful listening in your interactions with others. This means listening presently, without judgment, without immediately planning your response, and without assuming you already know what the other person is going to say. By truly listening, you open yourself up to new perspectives and insights that can dissolve ignorance.

Ask Questions: Instead of assuming you know the full story, ask questions. Curiosity is a powerful tool for transforming ignorance into understanding. In situations of conflict or confusion, approach the issue with a desire to learn rather than a desire to defend your position.

Educate Yourself: Make it a habit to seek out knowledge in areas where you feel uninformed. This could mean reading more about a particular topic, learning from experts, or engaging in conversations that challenge your current views. The more you know, the less likely you are to act from a place of ignorance.

Journaling: Think of a moment when you realized—perhaps in hindsight—that you didn't have all the facts, or that you'd been operating on a narrow understanding. Ask yourself:

- How did that limited perspective shape my decisions?
- What kept me from seeking more information or listening to another viewpoint?
- If I had been more open or curious, how might events have unfolded differently?

Reflect on one small step you could take to remain more open-minded in similar situations moving forward.

Cultivating Wisdom to Dissolve Ignorance

Ignorance may be a natural part of the human experience, but it doesn't have to control our lives. By cultivating awareness and openness, we can transform ignorance into wisdom, allowing us to approach life's challenges with clarity, understanding, and compassion. This wisdom not only helps us see all sides of a situation but also allows us to make better decisions and foster stronger, more harmonious relationships.

In both our personal and professional life, developing the wisdom to see beyond our limited perspective creates a more positive environment for ourselves and those around us. With greater awareness and openness, we respond to situations with insight rather than assumption, leading to outcomes that are more thoughtful, informed, and peaceful. Ignorance may cloud our vision at times, but with the practice of wisdom, we can always find our way back to the truth.

4

Ego

Pride, or Ego, is when we stand in a high place and look down on others, thinking we are better than they are.

In a vibrant city, there lived a young man named Leo who had climbed quickly up the ranks at his company. Known for his ambition, Leo took pride in his accomplishments, convinced that his success set him apart. Over time, his ego grew, making him see himself as invincible. He began to look down on his colleagues, dismissing their ideas and taking credit for their hard work, believing only his contributions truly mattered.

At home, his ego seeped into his relationships. His partner, Maya, noticed his growing arrogance, feeling less and less valued. Friends started drifting away, tired of Leo's self-centered conversations and his refusal to ask for help or admit mistakes. But Leo was too focused on maintaining his image of success to notice. His relentless pursuit of status left him stressed, struggling to sleep, and plagued by constant headaches. Yet he ignored these signs, confident he could handle everything on his own.

One day, after a major project went wrong at work, Leo found himself overwhelmed. For the first time, he couldn't find a solution, and his pride prevented him from asking for help. Frustrated and defeated, he returned home to find Maya packing a bag. "You don't need anyone, Leo," she said sadly. "Not your friend; not me. Your ego has taken up all the space."

Shocked and alone, Leo felt the weight of his choices. In desperation, he reached out to an old friend, who listened patiently and shared, "Ego is like a wall, Leo. It keeps others out, but it also traps you inside."

Leo's story illustrates the loneliness and self-deception that arise when Ego runs unchecked. By placing himself above everyone else, Leo lost sight of the genuine connections that truly make life fulfilling—reminding us that pride doesn't protect us, but instead builds walls that keep us from understanding, support, and growth.

Ego, one of the most powerful and deceptive of the Five Life Poisons, often leads to significant emotional and spiritual suffering. Ego is when we view ourselves as standing in a high place and looking down on others, thinking we are better than they are. The Ego can be seen as a form of Pride.

The feeling that we know what we are doing but others don't appreciate or value our knowledge and don't agree with us is an expression of Ego.

While it's natural and good to have a healthy sense of self, the Ego can become distorted and overinflated, leading us to develop a false sense of superiority, entitlement, or self-importance. Ego-driven behavior not only affects our inner peace, but it also influences how we relate to others and navigate the world around us. Understanding the emotions that arise from Ego, how our Ego impacts our relationships and work, what triggers our Ego reactions and defensiveness, and how to deflate our Ego, are the keys to cultivating humility, balance, and true self-awareness.

The Emotions of Ego: The Voice of Superiority and Insecurity

Ego often appears in one of two ways. It can puff us up with a sense of superiority. And it can act as a protective shield for our deepest insecurities. At its core, Ego creates a distorted view of our own importance, convincing us that we stand above others. And when Ego is hurt, Ego convinces us that we must guard ourselves against the fear of seeming inadequate or "less than" in their eyes.

When Ego runs high, we may find ourselves exuding a form of superiority that makes us feel our abilities outshine everyone else's. This can slide into outright arrogance, where we begin to believe our perspective is the only valid one, or into an attitude of entitlement, which assumes we deserve privileges others do not.

On the flip side, when Ego is hurt or offended, it can create feelings of insecurity. In those instances, what looks like supreme confidence is often a cover for an underlying fear of inadequacy or rejection. We might pour enormous energy into proving ourselves—personally or professionally—not because we are truly self-assured, but because we dread being overlooked.

This same tendency also explains why we may struggle to accept criticism or opposing viewpoints. If we're anxious about appearing small or unworthy, it can feel easier to dismiss new information or react defensively rather than risk having our vulnerabilities exposed. In reality, Ego's loud claims of self-importance can simply be a barrier erected out of fear—a shield that protects our pride but keeps us from genuine connection and understanding.

How Ego Affects Us and Those Around Us

Ego-driven behavior not only shapes how we feel internally, but also dictates how we interact with the people in our lives. It tends to distort relationships, create conflict, and stunt personal growth. In both personal and professional settings, an inflated Ego often generates friction and pushes others away.

In our closest relationships, Ego can morph into power struggles and misunderstandings, leaving real connection out of reach. The constant urge to be right—or to prove ourselves—makes it difficult to listen openly to what our partner, friends, or family have to say. Over time, this dynamic undermines trust and intimacy, as those who feel unheard withdraw emotionally.

Ego shows up in the workplace too, especially when we become overly concerned with how we appear or how our achievements compare to others. That anxiety can feed competitive or defensive behaviors, making true teamwork difficult. When leaders allow Ego to take the reins, they often stifle innovation and shut down new ideas, leaving employees feeling undervalued. A manager who clings to Ego may claim credit for a team's successes but point fingers at everyone else for failures, resulting in resentment and disheartened coworkers who feel their efforts are not valued.

What Triggers Ego Reactions and Defensiveness

Ego reactions—and the defensiveness that often accompanies them—commonly surface when we sense a threat to our self-image or our feeling of importance. Even routine feedback or criticism can make the Ego bristle if it suggests we might be wrong or less capable than we believe.

Faced with the possibility of error or inadequacy, the Ego instinctively wants to shield us from such an uncomfortable truth, so we may lash out or dismiss the critique altogether.

Comparisons to others can also inflame the Ego, particularly if we see someone else as more successful or better liked. This can spark jealousy, envy, or resentment, all of which come from the Ego's fear of being overshadowed.

Likewise, if we feel we aren't receiving the recognition or appreciation we deserve, the Ego may prompt us to seek attention through boasting or by putting others down. A threat to control—whether it's a plan falling apart or someone else taking the lead—can also stir up the Ego. It pushes us to regain authority through frustration or by refusing to compromise. Finally, fear of failure can magnify the Ego's influence. We may resist taking risks, deny our errors, or even blame others in an effort to protect the self-image we've grown attached to.

The Health Consequences of Ego

While anger flares quickly and attachment weighs us down over time, Ego introduces a stress response centered on preserving our self-image. When we feel pressured to appear infallible or superior, we keep our body in a near-constant state of tension. The effort required to maintain an inflated sense of self can lead to elevated cortisol levels—compromising our immune system and raising our risk for heart disease over the long term.[xi]

Ego also drives us to overextend ourselves, whether we are pushing for recognition at work, straining to outdo those around us, or refusing to acknowledge our own limits. This can result in burnout, leaving us exhausted and vulnerable to anxiety or depression.[xii] Further, the walls we build to protect our Ego can isolate us from supportive relationships, compounding loneliness and emotional stress.[xiii]

By learning to embrace humility and honest self-assessment, we can avoid the physical and emotional toll that Ego so often imposes.

The Root Cause of Ego

The root cause of Ego lies in a fundamental misunderstanding of the self. Often born from deep-seated insecurities, fears, and a hunger for external validation, Ego functions as a shield that protects us from feelings of inadequacy, rejection, or failure. By creating a false sense of superiority or invulnerability, it insulates us against the discomfort of acknowledging our own doubts.

One of the most common triggers for Ego is a genuine lack of self-confidence: when we don't feel adequate or "good enough," we sometimes inflate our sense of self to mask that unease, propping ourselves up with a defensive layer of pride or conceit.

Beyond insecurity, there is also a reluctance to appear vulnerable, which can push us to project a perfect image to the world. Admitting weaknesses or owning mistakes seems too risky, so we hide them behind the illusion of being infallible. This pattern deepens when we grow attached to seeking praise or approval, letting the opinions of others define our worth. Over time, the genuine self is overshadowed by the part of us that constantly craves recognition.

These patterns often take root early in life, when many of us are taught that success, status, and external rewards shape who we are. As we adopt these beliefs, the Ego's need for constant achievement and outside affirmation grows, further distancing us from true self-awareness and balance.

How to Deflate Ego and Reduce Pride

Deflating the Ego and reducing Pride calls for self-awareness, humility, and a shift away from chasing external validation or feeling superior. By working on these qualities, you can let go of Ego's hold and experience greater authenticity, balance, and peace in your life.

Develop Self-Awareness: Pay close attention to your emotions, thoughts, and reactions, especially when you feel defensive or superior. Ask yourself: *"What am I protecting? Which fear or insecurity is fueling this response?"* Pausing to reflect in this way lets you choose a more thoughtful reaction instead of an automatic, ego-driven one.

Practice Humility: Remind yourself that you are not above anyone else. Recognizing both your strengths and weaknesses without feeling a need to prove yourself opens you up to learning, collaboration, and genuine connection with others.

Acknowledge the Role of Others: When you're recognized or praised, share credit with the people who contributed to your success. Remember that you did not achieve this recognition solely by yourself and that luck, timing, or support played a part. Doing this helps keep you grounded and prevents the Ego from inflating.

Embrace Vulnerability: Allow yourself to be real with others by admitting mistakes or gaps in knowledge. Vulnerability dissolves the Ego's need for control or perfection, while drawing people closer to you through honesty and authenticity.

Seek Feedback: Invite input from those around you and remain open-minded when they share. Accepting feedback fosters humility and encourages ongoing growth, helping you step away from defensiveness and rigid viewpoints.

Practice Gratitude: Recognize the positive elements in your life—achievements, relationships, simple daily joys—and take a moment to appreciate them. This grateful mindset eases the drive for status or recognition, allowing you to stay present without comparing yourself to others.

Accept Imperfection: Recognize that you are not perfect—and that it's okay. Admitting your limitations makes you more willing to learn from others, seek help, and collaborate without feeling threatened, ultimately reducing pride and creating space for genuine development.

Journal: Think back to a recent situation where you felt defensive or overly proud.

- What was happening in that moment, and how did it make you feel?
- Can you identify any fears or insecurities that might have been driving your reaction?

Take a few minutes to write about the experience and consider how you could respond differently next time.

Transforming Ego with Humility

Ego, while a natural part of being human, becomes toxic when it drives us to act from a place of superiority, insecurity, or fear. It distorts our relationships, creates unnecessary conflict, and causes emotional and physical strain. However, by cultivating **humility** and **self-awareness**, we can begin to release the hold of Ego and connect more sincerely with others.

Humility allows us to embrace both our strengths and weaknesses without feeling the need to prove our worth. Self-awareness helps us recognize when Ego is in charge and choose a more appropriate response. Together, these qualities foster deeper, more meaningful relationships and create a sense of inner peace that is not dependent on external validation.

Releasing Ego doesn't mean diminishing our sense of self. It means freeing ourselves from false constructs that keep us bound to insecurity and fear. With time and practice, we can live with greater genuineness, compassion, and inner freedom, allowing the true self to emerge, free from Ego's illusions.

5

Jealousy

Jealousy is when we stand in a low place and look up at others, thinking we are not as good as they are.

In a vibrant town, there lived a man named Oliver who couldn't stand seeing others succeed. Whether it was a friend's new job, a neighbor's vacation, or even a distant cousin's happy relationship, Oliver felt a deep sting of jealousy. He masked it with polite smiles and congratulations, but inside, he'd think, "Why not me? Why do they get to be happy?"

As time passed, this jealousy grew like a shadow over Oliver's life. He stopped celebrating others' joys and began avoiding social gatherings, unable to bear witnessing anyone's happiness. His friends slowly drifted away, finding his negativity exhausting. Oliver soon felt isolated. Even his health began to suffer; he was constantly anxious, his sleep disturbed by a gnawing sense of dissatisfaction.

One evening, Oliver met a cheerful baker named Alma who invited him to join the weekly baking club. Reluctant at first, he decided to go, if only to distract himself. But as he watched Alma's joy in teaching others and sharing her recipes, something softened in him. Curious, he asked, "How are you so happy for others? Doesn't it ever make you less happy?"

Alma laughed. "Happiness isn't like a pie, Oliver. Just because someone else has a slice doesn't mean there's less for you. When you share in others' joy, it multiplies and brings joy back to you."

Oliver's struggle shows how jealousy can creep into our lives, eroding genuine connections and transforming celebrations into painful reminders of what we think we lack. By shying away from others' successes, he cut himself off from the very support and camaraderie he needed, revealing that jealousy doesn't just poison relationships—it isolates us from the abundant joys that can be found in shared happiness.

Jealousy, one of the most destructive of the Five Life Poisons, is a toxic emotion that can infiltrate all areas of life, distorting our relationships, self-perception, and well-being. Often referred to as the "green-eyed monster," Jealousy feeds on our feelings of inadequacy or fear of losing something valuable, whether it's love, success, or recognition. At its core, Jealousy is rooted in comparison and envy—comparing ourselves to others and feeling that we fall short. This comparison creates a sense of lacking, leaving us feeling unworthy or "less than," no matter how much we accomplish. Understanding what triggers jealousy and envy, how it affects our well-being and relationships, and the wisdom needed to calm this emotion is key to freeing ourselves from its grip.

The Emotions of Jealousy: The Green-Eyed Monster

Jealousy arises whenever we feel threatened by another person's achievements, relationships, status, or belongings. It might flare up when a friend accomplishes a goal we've worked toward, provoking that nagging question, "Why them and not me?"

In romantic relationships, it can surface the moment we sense our partner giving attention to someone else, triggering fear of rejection or worry that we're somehow inadequate.

At its core, jealousy can be a tangled mix of insecurity and self-doubt. We may feel unworthy or lacking in comparison to others, convincing ourselves that someone else's success leaves us with less. Over time, this mindset can reinforce the belief that we're simply not enough.

Jealousy also fuels resentment, driving us to begrudge others for having what we desire, until it becomes difficult to share in their happiness. In many cases, a deep-rooted fear of losing love, status, or attention underlies these emotions. That fear can push us to see others' gains as direct threats—leading us deeper into a cycle of jealousy that ultimately harms our relationships and our own sense of well-being.

What Triggers Jealousy?

Jealousy arises for many reasons, all tied to challenges in our self-worth or sense of security. One common trigger is the constant comparison we make between ourselves and others, whether through social media or face-to-face encounters. When we see someone else succeed, it can leave us feeling as though we're falling behind or missing out.

Fear of losing something valuable—such as a partner's affection or professional standing—is another key trigger. If someone new steps into the picture and achieves what we desire, we may react with heightened suspicion or insecurity. This becomes even more pronounced when our self-esteem is low; at those times, another person's success can magnify our own feelings of inadequacy.

Competitive environments can also fan the flames of jealousy, especially if we believe we're vying for the same accolades or affection. Past experiences of betrayal, rejection, or loss can leave us on guard for similar pain in the future, making us more prone to jealousy when any threat—real or perceived—surfaces again.

How Jealousy Affects Us and Those Around Us

Jealousy doesn't just stir up inner turmoil; it can also undermine our relationships and the environments we inhabit. In romantic partnerships, jealousy often breeds distrust, leads to controlling behaviors, and fosters emotional distance. The desire to keep tabs on a partner or question their motives can quickly erode intimacy and understanding, leaving each person feeling hurt or unappreciated. Among friends, jealousy might morph into resentment of a friend's achievements, lifestyle, or relationships, weakening bonds that were once supportive and warm.

In professional settings, jealousy can create a toxic work atmosphere. When we envy a colleague's success or recognition, we may engage in unhealthy competition, gossip, or attempts to sabotage their progress. This not only damages professional relationships but also distracts us from our own goals, as envy consumes our energy and attention. Over time, jealous feelings can diminish team morale and increase tension, negatively affecting both personal well-being and the overall workplace dynamic.

The Health Consequences of Jealousy

Jealousy combines elements of anger's intensity and attachment's fear of loss, creating a powerful blend of stress that can harm both our body and mind.

When we compare ourselves to others or fret about losing something important, our brain reacts by releasing cortisol.[xiv] Prolonged exposure to this stress hormone chips away at our immunity and raises our likelihood of developing heart-related issues.[xv]

Mentally, jealousy feeds on feelings of inadequacy and the belief that we are somehow "behind" or lacking. This drains our energy, eroding self-confidence and sometimes leading to anxiety or depression. We may find ourselves struggling to sleep as our mind replays fears of losing out or frets over someone else's achievements.

By practicing gratitude and self-acceptance, we can disrupt the cycle of jealousy and protect our emotional and physical health from its corrosive effects.

The Root Cause of Jealousy

At its heart, jealousy often arises from insecurity and comparison. When we feel uncertain about our own value, we naturally turn outward to measure our worth against others' successes, appearances, or relationships.

Each time we notice someone with more—more achievement, beauty, or recognition—we can't help but feel as though we fall short. This dynamic is rooted in low self-confidence; whenever we doubt our capabilities or fear we aren't as deserving, seeing someone else thrive only magnifies those worries.

Another key factor behind jealousy is the fear of losing something we hold dear, whether it's love, status, or acclaim. Anytime we sense a threat to these precious elements of our lives, Jealousy is stirred. Society's constant focus on comparison compounds the issue, too—on social media and in everyday interactions, we're inundated with glimpses of other people's accomplishments, fueling the idea that we're behind or lacking.

Compounding all of this is the notion of scarcity, the belief that there's only so much success or happiness to go around. When someone else triumphs, it feels as if there's less available for us, intensifying the pain of jealousy.

Why Does Comparison Hurt?

"Comparison is the thief of joy."
—Theodore Roosevelt

Comparison is a powerful catalyst for jealousy, often fueling emotional pain and dissatisfaction by reinforcing the belief that we're falling short. The moment we measure ourselves against others, we shift our focus away from what we do have and fixate on what we think is missing. This amplifies the gap between where we are and where we believe we should be, leading to frustration and a lingering sense of inadequacy.

Everyone's life path unfolds differently, and comparing ourselves to someone else ignores the fact that what they've achieved may not matter for our own happiness. When we judge our worth solely by another person's milestones, we lose sight of our unique strengths, personal growth, and individual experiences.

Finally, comparison often invites unrealistic expectations. This is especially obvious on social media, where images of beauty, fitness, and financial success can be exaggerated or entirely out of reach. Our behind-the-scenes struggles never seem to match these carefully curated highlight reels, leaving us discouraged—or even defeated—when we don't measure up to an illusion.

How to Stop Comparing with Others

Focus on Your Own Journey: Everyone has a unique path, and what works for someone else might not be right or necessary for you. Each time you catch yourself comparing your life, appearance, or success to someone else's, pause and remind yourself of the progress you've made. Reflect on what truly matters to you and celebrate your own milestones—even the small ones.

Limit (And Be Skeptical Of) Social Media Exposure: Social media often presents a carefully curated reality rather than the whole truth. If scrolling through other people's highlight reels makes you feel inadequate, consider setting time limits or taking breaks from platforms that trigger comparison. Remind yourself that online images of beautiful people can be digitally enhanced, and stories of apparently effortless success rarely capture the struggles and imperfections behind the scenes.

Cultivate Self-Compassion: When you're hard on yourself, comparing your perceived flaws to others' strengths becomes almost automatic. Instead, practice kindness toward yourself, especially in moments of insecurity. Acknowledge that everyone experiences doubts and remember that your worth isn't defined by how you stack up against someone else.

Practice Gratitude: Shifting your focus to what you do have—instead of what you believe you lack—can short-circuit the impulse to compare. By regularly recognizing the people, experiences, and small joys you're thankful for, you keep your attention on what enriches your life rather than on what seems missing.

Journal: Think back to a recent moment when you found yourself caught in a cycle of comparison.

- What specific thoughts or images triggered your envy or self-doubt?
- How did it feel in that moment, and how did you respond?

After reflecting on it, write about one step you can take to focus more on your own path the next time you sense comparison creeping in.

Transforming Jealousy With Self-Acceptance and Gratitude

Jealousy is a natural human emotion, yet it becomes toxic when it overshadows our thoughts, relationships, and actions. By fueling insecurity, fear, and resentment, it alienates us from others and robs us of inner peace.

The antidotes to jealousy are **self-acceptance** and **gratitude**—two qualities that help us find contentment within ourselves and appreciate what we already have.

Self-acceptance allows us to honor our own worth independent of external standards or others' accomplishments. When we embrace who we are and let go of endless comparisons, jealousy begins to lose its hold. We're then free to recognize our own unique strengths and no longer feel threatened by another person's success.

Gratitude complements self-acceptance by shifting our focus away from what we lack and toward all that we do have. When we regularly acknowledge the positive elements of our life—be they relationships, opportunities, or simple everyday joys—feelings of envy or comparison become easier to release.

Though jealousy may still emerge from time to time, self-acceptance and gratitude guide us back to a calm, more grounded place, keeping jealousy from dictating how we see ourselves or those around us.

6

Acknowledging the Five Life Poisons

A Path to Transformation

Recognizing when a Life Poison arises within us is essential. It's the first step toward breaking the cycle of suffering and imbalance these poisons create. Whether it's Anger, Jealousy, Ego, Ignorance, or Attachment, these emotions naturally come up time and again in our lives. The goal is not to suppress or deny them but to notice when they appear, pause, and then apply the appropriate wisdom before reacting.

When we sense a Life Poison surfacing, we try stepping back to observe what's happening inside instead of immediately acting on our emotions. In that space between feeling the poison and responding to it, real transformation can take hold. By creating this pause, we give ourselves the chance to choose a wiser, more balanced path—rather than an impulsive or reactive one.

It's tempting to say, "I'm not a jealous person" or "I'm not attached to people or things," yet these Five Life Poisons are often subtle and pervasive. They can shape the way we think, behave, and connect with others—sometimes without our conscious awareness. Genuinely understanding their impact requires us to pause, reflect, and acknowledge how we feel in relation to each poison.

Take anger as an example. Our first instinct might be to lash out or become defensive. However, the moment we recognize anger as a poison clouding our perception, we can pause and ask, "*Where is this coming from? Is it fear, frustration, or something else? Which antidote—compassion, patience, understanding—will bring clarity right now?*" By using that reflective pause, we reclaim power from the poison and create a more peaceful outcome for yourself and those around you.

Spending real time contemplating your reactions to each of the Five Life Poisons is the key to lasting change. We may not think of ourselves as ruled by Anger, Jealousy, or Attachment, yet a closer look could reveal hints—or even strong currents—of one or more poisons influencing our mindset and actions. Simply acknowledging their presence provides the awareness we need to use wisdom as an antidote whenever they arise.

How to Start the Journey of Transformation

Starting the journey of acknowledging and addressing the Five Life Poisons can feel overwhelming. With intentional steps, we can begin to bring awareness and healing into our life. Here's how to begin:

1. **Set Aside Time for Reflection**: Commit to giving yourself a quiet space for contemplation so you can recognize when a Life Poison is present. Even ten to fifteen minutes of daily reflection can make a difference. During this time, consider journaling your emotions and thoughts related to each Poison.

2. **Focus on One Poison at a Time**: Rather than trying to address all the Poisons at once, pick one to concentrate on. Spend a week noticing how it appears in your life and pay close attention to how it makes you feel. If you've chosen Jealousy, for instance, write down the thoughts that come up whenever it arises and see if you notice any patterns.

3. **Acknowledge the Reactions**: A pivotal step in transformation is acknowledging how each Poison affects you. When a surge of anger, jealousy, or attachment surfaces, pause and observe your reaction. Avoid judging yourself for feeling these emotions; simply recognize that they exist. This nonjudgmental awareness helps shift from impulsive reactions to more thoughtful responses.

4. **Contemplate the Impact**: Ask yourself how the Poison you're focusing on influences not just your own mindset but also the people around you. Does Anger

create tension in your relationships? Does Attachment lead to stress? Seeing the wider effects of these Poisons can strengthen your resolve to change.

5. **Apply Wisdom**: Once you've identified how each Poison shows up, use the appropriate antidote. If jealousy flares up, practice gratitude. If you catch yourself acting out of ego, practice humility. Little by little, you'll develop a habit of replacing negative patterns with healthier, more constructive responses.

6. **Track Your Progress**: Keep a journal of your observations and insights. Each time you notice a Poison and respond with wisdom, record it. Seeing these moments written down will motivate you and serve as a reminder of your growth over time.

The Power of Contemplation: A Week for Each Poison

Consider dedicating a full week to each Life Poison, giving yourself intentional time for self-reflection and deeper insight:

Week 1: Anger. Observe when anger arises. What triggers it, and how does it affect you and others? Practice patience and calm as antidotes to anger.

Week 2: Ignorance. Reflect on what you avoid learning about or facing head-on. Where can you open your mind to new perspectives? Practice awareness and openness.

Week 3: Pride (Ego). Notice moments when pride or ego takes over. Pause, step back, and respond with humility. Focus on collaboration and genuinely listening to others.

Week 4: Jealousy. Tune in to any feelings of jealousy. How does comparison feed those feelings? Practice gratitude for what you already have and embrace self-acceptance to soothe the green-eyed monster.

Week 5: Attachment. Pay attention to where you feel most attached. What are you afraid to lose? Practice non-attachment by welcoming change and allowing life to flow.

At the end of each week, take a few moments to write down what you've discovered about yourself. Note how each poison influences your life and the ways you've applied wisdom to transform that poison into a source of clarity and peace.

The Journey to Nurture Mind, Body, and Spirit

This journey of self-reflection is about much more than simply naming the Five Life Poisons. It's an opportunity to nurture your mind, body, and spirit.

As you become aware of each poison, you'll start noticing how subtly—and powerfully—they can influence your relationships, your well-being, and even your professional life. The deeper you delve into understanding these poisons, the more profound your transformation can be.

By committing to this process, you tap into your inner self, discovering that genuine change not only alters how you view your own life but also affects the people closest to you. Friends, family, and colleagues will sense the shift as you become more balanced, more present, and more in control of your reactions. This transformation reshapes not just how you feel, but also how you interact with others, fostering healthier and more harmonious connections.

As you release the grip of the Five Life Poisons and apply wisdom in their place, you'll gain clarity, emotional freedom, and a deeper sense of purpose. This change has the power to reshape your life in ways you might never have imagined.

It's important to remember, though, that these Five Life Poisons won't vanish completely; they're part of the human experience. Still, when you recognize their signs, you can keep them from hijacking your actions and decisions. Over time, the more consistently you practice awareness, the easier it becomes to replace these poisons with wisdom, bringing more balance, health, and harmony to every aspect of your life.

Of course, this transformation doesn't happen overnight. It requires patience and steady effort. Yet with each moment of heightened awareness and applied wisdom, you'll become stronger in handling these emotions—ultimately finding yourself with a calmer mind, better emotional balance, and a life infused with greater peace and clarity.

7

Applying Wisdom as the Antidote

Applying wisdom means taking mindful action grounded in understanding and awareness. Each of the Five Life Poisons has a corresponding antidote that fosters greater balance and clarity. Here's how you can begin using these antidotes to counteract each poison:

Anger → Patience and Compassion: When anger surfaces, pause and take a few deep breaths before reacting. Ask yourself what triggered the anger in the first place. By practicing patience, you allow the intensity of the emotion to subside rather than fueling it. At the same time, extend compassion—to both yourself and anyone involved—acknowledging that anger often springs from deeper pain or frustration.

Ignorance → Awareness and Openness: Ignorance dissolves when you recognize your own limited perspective. First, become aware that you lack knowledge of some area or thing. Make a conscious effort to learn, whether that means seeking new information or being open to different cultures and experiences. Curiosity and a willingness to grow will naturally replace narrow thinking with wisdom.

Ego → Humility and Gratitude: When your ego starts to inflate—wanting to be right, superior, or validated—pause and remember that true strength lies in collaboration and continual learning. Show gratitude for others' contributions and insights to defuse the need for personal recognition.

Jealousy → Self-Acceptance and Gratitude: If you catch yourself feeling jealous, step back and remind yourself that your worth isn't determined by anyone else's success. Cultivate gratitude for your own blessings, however small. By shifting your focus from what you believe you lack to what you genuinely have, you invite a sense of contentment.

Attachment → Non-Attachment and Acceptance: When you notice yourself clinging to a person, object, or outcome, remember that everything is impermanent. Embrace each moment without trying to freeze it in place and accept that change is a natural part of life. Practicing non-attachment doesn't mean you disengage; it simply means you cherish life's flow without trying to hold on too tightly.

By applying these antidotes consistently, you'll begin to see your reactions transform—from negative patterns to positive, conscious choices. Over time, the poisons lose their sway, and you gain greater freedom in how you respond to life's inevitable ups and downs.

Putting It into Practice

Emma was in the middle of a project at work that she had poured her heart into. She had spent countless hours refining her ideas and was excited to present her progress to her team. However, just days before the final presentation, a colleague, Alex, presented a similar idea as his own, without acknowledging Emma's contributions. Her heart sank, and she felt an immediate rush of anger and resentment. How could he take credit for something she had worked so hard on?

The first poison, Anger, surged within her, filling her thoughts with frustration. The situation felt deeply unfair. But then she took a deep breath and paused, deciding to lean into compassion rather than react impulsively. As she centered herself, she realized that reacting with anger would only escalate the situation and cause more division. She reminded herself that she didn't truly know Alex's intentions—perhaps he hadn't even realized the overlap. Compassion allowed her to view the situation with a calmer heart, giving her the space to respond rather than react.

Next, she noticed Ignorance creeping in as assumptions filled her mind. She assumed that Alex's intentions were selfish, but she caught herself and decided to give him the benefit of the doubt. She didn't know his perspective, nor did she know his challenges. This awareness allowed her to approach him with an open mind. Instead of jumping to conclusions, she compassionately reminded herself to seek understanding before judgment.

Emma also felt a rise in Ego as she thought about her hard work. The idea of not receiving credit bruised her pride, making her want to protect her status. But, practicing compassion, she recognized that her ego was clinging to her need for validation. She realized that Alex's recognition didn't define her value or the quality of her work. Compassion helped her see beyond her own need for acknowledgment and opened her heart to the bigger picture: the project's success and the team's collective growth.

When she heard positive feedback directed at Alex for his presentation, Emma couldn't help but feel Jealousy. It stung to see others praise him for something she felt was rightfully hers. But rather than letting jealousy fester, she reminded herself of her values. Compassion showed her that genuine support and kindness were far more rewarding than harboring jealousy. She congratulated Alex inwardly, knowing that her time for recognition would come when she acted with integrity.

Finally, she felt Attachment to the idea of being seen as the sole contributor to the project. She was deeply invested in her role, and this attachment made her feel protective, even possessive. However, by bringing compassion into the mix, she gently reminded herself that the project's purpose was more than her own success. Releasing her attachment to individual ownership allowed her to feel lighter, more collaborative, and open to shared success.

With these shifts in her mindset, Emma approached Alex calmly and shared her contributions. She expressed her excitement about the overlap in their ideas and suggested ways they could integrate both perspectives. Alex was taken aback by her kindness, admitting he hadn't realized how similar his presentation was to hers and apologizing for the oversight. Together, they found ways to strengthen the project, incorporating each other's ideas and skills.

Through the compassion she extended toward herself and others, Emma was able to transform what could have been a toxic and divisive experience into one of collaboration and understanding. She saw how defusing the Five Life Poisons with compassion brought a deeper sense of peace, clarity, and connection—not only with Alex but also with herself.

By the end of the project, Emma felt a profound sense of fulfillment, not just from the work she contributed but from the growth and kindness she had shown along the way.

Emma's experience shows how quickly the Five Life Poisons can appear in our daily interactions and how even a single shift in attitude—rooted in awareness and compassion—can transform a conflict into a powerful opportunity for understanding, collaboration, and growth.

How to Apply These Principles to Modern Life

Applying wisdom to address and transform the Five Life Poisons—Anger, Ignorance, Ego, Jealousy, and Attachment—calls for consistent self-awareness, reflection, and mindful action.

Each poison can subtly shape your life, and only through dedicated practice can you replace negative patterns with positive growth.

Step 1: Self-Awareness – Recognize the Poisons as They Arise

Your first priority is to cultivate self-awareness. You can't transform what you don't acknowledge, so start by noticing when one of the Five Life Poisons influences your thoughts, emotions, or behavior.

How to Practice:
- Observe your emotional reactions to daily events. The moment you feel angry, insecure, or envious, pause and take a few slow breaths.
- Ask yourself, "What am I feeling right now? Which Poison is behind this reaction?"
- Consider keeping a journal and noting each episode. Identifying the emotion and any related Poison helps you see patterns over time, making it easier to recognize them in the future.

Step 2: Acknowledge Without Judgment

Once you identify a Life Poison, acknowledge it kindly. It's normal to feel anger, jealousy, or attachment; you don't need to judge yourself for these emotions. This compassionate acknowledgment creates room for genuine transformation.

How to Practice:
- When you notice a Poison at work, simply say, "I see that I'm feeling angry (or jealous, attached, etc.), and that's okay." Then remind yourself you have the power to choose how to respond.

- Practice self-compassion. Recognize that these emotions are part of being human, and that learning to manage them is an ongoing process.

Step 3: Pause and Create Space Before Reacting

Before reacting to the Life Poison, take a brief pause. This moment of stillness allows you to choose a thoughtful response rather than an impulsive one, giving wisdom a chance to emerge.

How to Practice:
- When you sense Anger, Jealousy, or Ego flaring up, take a few deep, calming breaths before speaking or acting.
- Ask yourself, "Is my reaction coming from fear, insecurity, or comparison? What would be a more compassionate response right now?"

Step 4: Apply the Antidotes of Wisdom

Refer back to the antidotes you've learned for each Poison—patience for Anger, awareness for Ignorance, humility for Ego, and so on. Familiarize yourself with these practices and integrate them into your daily life.

Step 5: Practice Mindfulness

Mindfulness keeps you present, helping you observe your emotions without being swept away. By weaving mindfulness into your daily routine, you'll more easily spot a Life Poison and respond with clarity rather than reactivity.

How to Practice:
- Start your day with a brief mindfulness session. Focus on your breath, gently noting any thoughts that arise without judgment.
- At various moments throughout the day, pause to check in with yourself. Notice if you're tense, angry, or anxious, and then choose a wise, compassionate response.

Step 6: Reflect and Grow

Transformation is gradual. Regular reflection helps you see what's working and where you may need more practice.

How to Practice:
- At the end of each day or week, set aside time to reflect on your emotional experiences.
- Write about moments when you successfully applied wisdom and times when you struggled. Over time, you'll gain deeper insight into your triggers and develop stronger habits of responding wisely.

Step 7: Stay Committed to the Practice

Overcoming the Five Life Poisons is a lifelong journey. Commitment and patience are essential. As you hone your awareness and practice using wisdom, you'll notice these Poisons lose their grip, allowing you greater peace and balance.

How to Practice:
- When you slip into old patterns, acknowledge it gently—no self-judgment. Congratulate yourself for realizing you've slipped into an unwanted pattern. Reaffirm your intention to respond with wisdom next time.
- Surround yourself with reminders of your commitment: read inspiring books, engage with like-minded communities, and continually explore new ways to nurture personal growth.

By consistently applying these steps, you'll discover that the Five Life Poisons gradually loosen their hold, and you'll develop a more peaceful, resilient approach to life's challenges.

The Happiness Response

We've seen how each Life Poison can keep our mind and body in a cycle of stress and conflict. However, there is a powerful counterbalance, known as "The Happiness Response."

By choosing positivity over negativity—through compassion, self-awareness, humility, and other antidotes—we create harmony within ourselves and with the world around us, fostering resilience, growth, and peace.

When we apply the antidotes to each poison—compassion for Anger, awareness for Ignorance, humility for Ego, gratitude for Jealousy, and non-attachment for Attachment—our brain's capacity for neuroplasticity comes into play. Over time, this mindful practice builds new neural pathways, reinforcing more balanced emotional responses and healthier thought patterns.[xvi]

Instead of constantly fueling the release of stress hormones, as we adopt these wisdoms, our bodies begin to release "happiness hormones," a biochemical shift that reinforces our emotional and physical transformation. Dopamine, often called the "reward chemical," is released when we achieve goals or engage in self-reflection. Replacing attachment with contentment fosters dopamine production, reinforcing feelings of fulfillment and motivation.[xvii] Serotonin, the "mood stabilizer," increases when we practice gratitude and connect with others.[xviii] Oxytocin, known as the "love hormone," is stimulated through acts of kindness and compassion, enhancing social bonds and reducing stress.[xix] Endorphins, natural painkillers, are released during physical activities and laughter, promoting relaxation and vitality.[xx]

As these hormones flow more freely, we begin to experience deeper, restorative sleep and notice a boost in our immune function.[xxi] Emotionally, releasing the Life Poisons in favor of wisdom fosters clearer thinking, sharper problem-solving, and greater resilience. We can navigate life's challenges with more grace, confident that our well-being won't be derailed by sudden surges of anger, jealousy, or ego-driven anxiety.

Embracing the Happiness Response is ultimately a declaration of self-love and self-respect. By replacing each Life Poison with its antidote, we cultivate a life filled with peace, purpose, and vitality—one that radiates positivity to those around us. As we continue to nurture this response, we honor our mind, body, and spirit, creating a solid foundation for a healthier, more harmonious existence.

Conclusion: Embrace the Journey of Transformation

Applying these principles to modern life is not about perfection—it's about progress. The first step is understanding the Life Poisons, seeing how they arise and influence your thoughts, feelings, and actions.

Once you become aware of their presence, you can recognize the harm they cause, then apply the appropriate wisdom to reduce their impact. Remember, this isn't an overnight fix; consistent practice, patience, and awareness are key.

Every time you pause before reacting, every moment of mindfulness, and every application of compassion, humility, or non-attachment helps loosen the grip of these poisons. As you continue on this path, you'll find your relationships deepen, your inner calm grows, and your overall well-being flourishes.

Embrace the journey, remain patient, and allow your ongoing practice to guide you toward lasting transformation—one breath, one choice, and one kind thought at a time.

The Continued Journey

The path to understanding and transforming the Five Life Poisons is a lifelong endeavor. My hope is that this book has offered you helpful insights as you learn to recognize these poisons, navigate their influence, and discover the power of wisdom-based practices. With consistent attention and patience, you can continue moving toward deeper healing and growth.

If you have questions or need further support, feel free to reach out to me anytime via email. I'd love to hear about your progress and how the book has been part of your journey. **deborah@annapurnabluewellness.com**.

To enrich your exploration, I'm pleased to offer a companion workbook that more deeply explores how we manage the Five Life Poisons. You can find it by visiting **annapurnabluewellness.com** and joining our "Five Life Poisons Membership." Use code **110524** for a complimentary digital copy of the workbook. As a member, you'll also gain access to a community of individuals committed to overcoming life's challenges and transforming negativity.

I invite you, too, to consider experiencing an AnnapurnaBlue Wellness Retreat in person. We'd be delighted to welcome you as we continue learning, growing, and finding peace together. Thank you for letting this book be part of your journey.

About Deborah Peteler

If you know Deborah Peteler, you'll quickly discover that she just likes to be "Deborah"—casual, grounded, and most comfortable in her favorite T-shirt and jeans. An adventure enthusiast at heart, Deborah's passion for travel takes her far beyond U.S. borders, immersing her in diverse cultures and lessons that enrich both her life and her work. She is deeply devoted to her family and friends, finding immense joy in these connections.

But there is so much more to Deborah. With over thirty years of education and experience, she masterfully blends ancient Tibetan healing wisdom with modern Western modalities, creating a unique and effective approach to holistic wellness. As a dedicated therapist and life coach, she specializes in trauma recovery and life transformation, offering nurturing and healing that encompasses the mind, body, and spirit.

As the co-founder of AnnapurnaBlue Wellness, Deborah hosts wellness retreats worldwide, inspired by her transformative work with the Five Life Poisons. Her award-winning programs have empowered countless students to learn, heal, and transform their lives. Beyond AnnapurnaBlue, she also serves as the director of Yeru Bön Center, a center dedicated to preserving ancient Tibetan spiritual wisdom and healing, under the guidance of her teacher and the center's founder, Latri Nyima Dakpa Rinpoche.

This work is not just a hobby for Deborah—it is her life's purpose to be of service to others. Over the past three years, she has recovered from a life-threatening health condition, and during her recovery, she made the conscious choice to devote her purpose to helping others. Through her personal experience with healing, she has become even more committed to guiding people to live lives of goodness, purpose, and a daily passion for wellness.

Her dedication, resilience, and deep knowledge make her a true force for wellness. Her journey is not just about healing herself, but about helping others find their own path to well-being, transformation, and empowerment.

Notes

[i] Wharton, E., & Kanas, N. (2019). Mindfulness-Based Stress Reduction for the Treatment of Anxiety Disorders. International Journal of Group Psychotherapy, 69, 362 - 372. https://www.tandfonline.com/doi/full/10.1080/00207284.2019.1599289.

[ii] Grewal, D. (2014). Improving Concentration and Mindfulness in Learning through Meditation. IOSR Journal of Humanities and Social Science, 19, 33-39. http://www.iosrjournals.org/iosr-jhss/papers/Vol19-issue2/Version-5/F019253339.pdf.

[iii] Jeong, J., Zanuzzi, M., Dacosta, D., Li, S., & Park, J. (2024). Mindfulness-Based Stress Reduction and Autonomic Modulation in Chronic Kidney Disease. Physiology. https://journals.physiology.org/doi/abs/10.1152/physiol.2024.39.S1.706.

Ngô, T. (2013). [Review of the effects of mindfulness meditation on mental and physical health and its mechanisms of action]. Sante mentale au Quebec, 38 2, 19-34.

Kabat-Zinn, J., Lipworth, L., & Burney, R. (1985). The clinical use of mindfulness meditation for the self-regulation of chronic pain.

Journal of Behavioral Medicine, 8, 163-190. https://link.springer.com/article/10.1007/BF00845519.

Raevuori, A. (2016). Health effects of mindfulness - what should the doctor know?. Duodecim; laaketieteellinen aikakauskirja, 132 20, 1890-7.

[iv] Burgess, S., & Saxton, T. (2012). Adult anger management.

McCarty, R. (2016). The Fight-or-Flight Response: A Cornerstone of Stress Research. , 33-37. https://www.sciencedirect.com/science/article/abs/pii/B9780128009512000042.

Sapkota, N. (2017). Anger;it's impact on human body. , 5, 3-5.

[v] Bunnett, N. (2005). The stressed gut: contributions of intestinal stress peptides to inflammation and motility.. Proceedings of the National Academy of Sciences of the United States of America, 102 21, 7409-10. https://www.pnas.org/doi/full/10.1073/pnas.0503092102.

[vi] Yadav, I., Wakode, S., & Khasimbi, S. (2023). The role of stress in the development of cardiovascular diseases. *Journal of Nursing & Healthcare*. https://www.opastpublishers.com/open-access-articles/the-role-of-stress-in-the-development-of-cardiovascular-diseases.pdf.

[vii] Gouin, J., Kiecolt-Glaser, J., Malarkey, W., & Glaser, R. (2008). The influence of anger expression on wound healing. Brain, Behavior, and Immunity, 22, 699-708. https://www.sciencedirect.com/science/article/abs/pii/S0889159107002644.

Tsuboi, H., Hamer, M., Tanaka, G., Takagi, K., Kinae, N., & Steptoe, A. (2008). Responses of ultra-weak chemiluminescence and secretory IgA in saliva to the induction of angry and depressive moods. *Brain, Behavior, and Immunity*, 22, 209-214.

https://www.sciencedirect.com/science/article/abs/pii/S0889159107001699.

[viii] Krizan, Z., & Hisler, G. (2019). Sleepy anger: Restricted sleep amplifies angry feelings.. Journal of experimental psychology. General, 148 7, 1239-1250 . https://psycnet.apa.org/doiLanding?doi=10.1037%2Fxge0000522.

Hisler, G. (2016). Aggressiveness and sleep: People with quick tempers and less anger control have objectively worse sleep quality. https://dr.lib.iastate.edu/entities/publication/35f4df95-625c-41db-9fea-1cdc5b62fa95.

Jaremka, L., Glaser, R., Loving, T., Malarkey, W., Stowell, J., & Kiecolt-Glaser, J. (2013). Attachment Anxiety Is Linked to Alterations in Cortisol Production and Cellular Immunity. *Psychological Science*, 24, 272 - 279. https://journals.sagepub.com/doi/10.1177/0956797612452571.

[ix] Benschop, R., Brosschot, J., Godaert, G., Smet, M., Geenen, R., Olff, M., Heijnen, C., & Ballieux, R. (1994). Chronic stress affects immunologic but not cardiovascular responsiveness to acute psychological stress in humans.. The American journal of physiology, 266 1 Pt 2, R75-80 . https://journals.physiology.org/doi/abs/10.1152/ajpregu.1994.266.1.R75.

Kario, K., McEwen, B., & Pickering, T. (2003). Disasters and the heart: a review of the effects of earthquake-induced stress on cardiovascular disease.. Hypertension research : official journal of the Japanese Society of Hypertension, 26 5, 355-67. https://www.jstage.jst.go.jp/article/hypres/26/5/26_5_355/_article.

[x] De Berker, A., Rutledge, R., Mathys, C., Marshall, L., Cross, G., Dolan, R., & Bestmann, S. (2016). Computations of uncertainty mediate acute stress responses in humans. *Nature Communications*, 7. https://www.nature.com/articles/ncomms10996.

Brosschot, J., Verkuil, B., & Thayer, J. (2016). The default response to uncertainty and the importance of perceived safety in anxiety and stress: An evolution-theoretical perspective.. *Journal of anxiety disorders*, 41, 22-34 . https://www.sciencedirect.com/science/article/abs/pii/S0887618516 300585.

[xi] Cheng, J., Tracy, J., & Miller, G. (2013). Are narcissists hardy or vulnerable? The role of narcissism in the production of stress-related biomarkers in response to emotional distress.. *Emotion*, 13 6, 1004-11. https://psycnet.apa.org/doiLanding?doi=10.1037%2Fa0034410.

Khan, M. (2006). Chapter 84 - Stress and Heart Disease., 569-573. https://www.sciencedirect.com/science/article/abs/pii/B978012406 0616500862.

[xii] Lambie, G. (2007). The Contribution of Ego Development Level to Burnout in School Counselors: Implications for Professional School Counseling.. *Journal of Counseling and Development*, 85, 82-88. https://onlinelibrary.wiley.com/doi/10.1002/j.1556-6678.2007.tb00447.x.

[xiii] Bedan, V. (2020). Psychological characteristics of the types of the experience of loneliness functional orientation. *EUROPEAN HUMANITIES STUDIES: State and Society*. https://ehs.eeipsy.org/index.php/ehs/article/view/207.

Campagne, D. (2019). Stress and perceived social isolation (loneliness).. *Archives of gerontology and geriatrics*, 82, 192-199. https://www.sciencedirect.com/science/article/abs/pii/S0167494319 300433.

[xiv] Smith, T., & Jordan, K. (2015). Interpersonal motives and social-evaluative threat: Effects of acceptance and status stressors on cardiovascular reactivity and salivary cortisol response. *Psychophysiology*, 52 2, 269-76 . https://onlinelibrary.wiley.com/doi/10.1111/psyp.12318.

[xv] Friedman, E., Karlamangla, A., Almeida, D., & Seeman, T. (2010). Social Conflict and Cortisol Regulation.

[xvi] Roemer, L., Williston, S., & Rollins, L. (2015). Mindfulness and emotion regulation. *Current opinion in psychology*, 3, 52-57. https://www.sciencedirect.com/science/article/abs/pii/S2352250X15000974.

Guendelman, S., Medeiros, S., & Rampes, H. (2017). Mindfulness and Emotion Regulation: Insights from Neurobiological, Psychological, and Clinical Studies. *Frontiers in Psychology*, 8. https://www.frontiersin.org/journals/psychology/articles/10.3389/fpsyg.2017.00220/full.

[xvii] Liu, S. (2020). What Drives Us? Chasing Reward in a Dopaminergic Society. , 11. https://journals.library.columbia.edu/index.php/cusj/article/view/5654.

Herd, S., Mingus, B., & O'Reilly, R. (2010). Dopamine and self-directed learning. , 58-63. https://ebooks.iospress.nl/publication/6223.

[xviii] Kiser, D., Steemers, B., Branchi, I., & Homberg, J. (2012). The reciprocal interaction between serotonin and social behaviour. *Neuroscience & Biobehavioral Reviews*, 36, 786-798. https://www.sciencedirect.com/science/article/abs/pii/S0149763411002168.

Watkins, P. (2014). Does Gratitude Enhance Social Well-Being?. , 139-157. https://link.springer.com/chapter/10.1007/978-94-007-7253-3_8.

[xix] Olff, M. (2012). Bonding after trauma: on the role of social support and the oxytocin system in traumatic stress. *European Journal*

of Psychotraumatology, 3.
https://www.tandfonline.com/doi/full/10.3402/ejpt.v3i0.18597

Kucerova, B., Levit-Binnun, N., Gordon, I., & Golland, Y. (2023). From Oxytocin to Compassion: The Saliency of Distress. *Biology*, 12. https://www.mdpi.com/2079-7737/12/2/183.

[xx] Cohen, E., Ejsmond-Frey, R., Knight, N., & Dunbar, R. (2010). Rowers' high: behavioural synchrony is correlated with elevated pain thresholds. *Biology Letters*, 6, 106 - 108. https://royalsocietypublishing.org/doi/10.1098/rsbl.2009.0670.

Kalaivani, S., & Rajkumar, K. (2017). Laughter is the best medicine for stress relief. *International Journal of Advances in Nursing Management*, 5, 262-264. https://www.indianjournals.com/ijor.aspx?target=ijor:ijanm&volume=5&issue=3&article=016.

[xxi] Besedovsky, L., Lange, T., & Born, J. (2011). Sleep and immune function. *Pflügers Archiv - European Journal of Physiology*, 463, 121 - 137. https://link.springer.com/article/10.1007/s00424-011-1044-0.

Lange, T. (2016). SP0046 Sleep as A Modulator and Adjuvant in Immunity. *Annals of the Rheumatic Diseases*, 75, 13 - 13. https://ard.eular.org/article/S0003-4967(24)56424-X/pdf.

www.ingramcontent.com/pod-product-compliance
Lightning Source LLC
Chambersburg PA
CBHW060536080526
44586CB00012B/748